Maya Angelou _____ ait___, singer, actress, dancer, activist, editor, fil_____ ' ° r ter, mother, and inaugural poet. She first thrilled the ____ with her autobiography *I Know Why the Caged Bird Sings*. This was followed by *Gather Together in My Name*, *Singin' and Swingin' and Gettin' Merry Like Christmas*, *The Heart of a Woman*, *All God's Children Need Travelling Shoes* and in 2002 the sixth and final volume, *A Song Flung Up to Heaven*. She has written two collections of prose, *Wouldn't Take Nothing for My Journey Now* and *Even the Stars Look Lonesome*. She has also written six poetry collections, as well as the inaugural poem for President Clinton, and a cookbook, *Hallelujah! The Welcome Table*, all of which are published by Virago. Maya Angelou now has a lifetime appointment as Reynolds Professor of American Studies at Wake Forest University of North Carolina.

Maya Angelou

And Still I Rise

Virago

VIRAGO

This edition published 2003
Reprinted 2007

First published by Virago Press 1986
Reprinted 1988, 1990, 1992, 1993, 1995, 1997, 1998, 1999

And Still I Rise copyright © by Maya Angelou 1978
Shaker, Why Don't You Sing? copyright © by
Maya Angelou 1983
This arrangement, *And Still I Rise*, copyright © by
Maya Angelou 1986

*A CIP catalogue for this book is
available from the British Library*

This Virago edition, *And Still I Rise*, is made up of two of
Maya Angelou's collections of poetry, previously available
only in the USA and Canada: *And Still I Rise* (1978) and
Shaker, Why Don't You Sing? (1983) which were published by
Random House, Inc., New York, and Random House of
Canada Limited, Toronto

ISBN 978-0-86068-757-3

Papers used by Virago are natural, recyclable products made from
wood grown in sustainable forests and certified in accordance with
the rules of the Forest Stewardship Council.

Printed and bound in Great Britain by Clays Ltd, St Ives plc
Paper supplied by Hellefoss AS, Norway

Virago Press
An imprint of
Little, Brown Book Group
Brettenham House
Lancaster Place
London WC2E 7EN

A Member of the Hachette Livre Group of Companies

www.virago.co.uk

CONTENTS

AND STILL I RISE

SHAKER WHY DON'T YOU SING?

AND
STILL
I RISE

This book is dedicated to a
few of the Good Guys

You to laugh with
You to cry to
I can just about make
it over

JESSICA MITFORD
GERARD W. PURCELL
JAY ALLEN

PART ONE

Touch Me, Life, Not Softly

A KIND OF LOVE, SOME SAY

Is it true the ribs can tell
The kick of a beast from a
Lover's fist? The bruised
Bones recorded well
The sudden shock, the
Hard impact. Then swollen lids,
Sorry eyes, spoke not
Of lost romance, but hurt.

Hate often is confused. Its
Limits are in zones beyond itself. And
Sadists will not learn that
Love by nature, exacts a pain
Unequalled on the rack.

COUNTRY LOVER

Funky blues
Keen toed shoes
High water pants
Saddy night dance
Red soda water
and anybody's daughter

REMEMBRANCE

for Paul

Your hands easy
weight, teasing the bees
hived in my hair, your smile at the
slope of my cheek. On the
occasion, you press
above me, glowing, spouting
readiness, mystery rapes
my reason.

When you have withdrawn
your self and the magic, when
only the smell of your
love lingers between
my breasts, then, only
then, can I greedily consume
your presence.

WHERE WE BELONG, A DUET

In every town and village,
In every city square,
In crowded places
I searched the faces
Hoping to find
Someone to care.

I read mysterious meanings
In the distant stars,
Then I went to schoolrooms
And poolrooms
And half-lighted cocktail bars.
Braving dangers,
Going with strangers,
I don't even remember their names.
I was quick and breezy
And always easy
Playing romantic games.

I wined and dined a thousand exotic Joans and Janes
In dusty dance halls, at debutante balls,
On lonely country lanes.
I fell in love forever,
Twice every year or so.
I wooed them sweetly, was theirs completely,
But they always let me go.
Saying bye now, no need to try now,

You don't have the proper charms.
Too sentimental and much too gentle
I don't tremble in your arms.

Then you rose into my life
Like a promised sunrise.
Brightening my days with the light in your eyes.
I've never been so strong,
Now I'm where I belong.

PHENOMENAL WOMAN

Pretty women wonder where my secret lies.
I'm not cute or built to suit a fashion model's size
But when I start to tell them,
They think I'm telling lies.
I say,
It's in the reach of my arms,
The span of my hips,
The stride of my step,
The curl of my lips.
I'm a woman
Phenomenally.
Phenomenal woman,
That's me.

I walk into a room
Just as cool as you please,
And to a man,
The fellows stand or
Fall down on their knees.
Then they swarm around me,
A hive of honey bees.
I say,
It's the fire in my eyes,
And the flash of my teeth,
The swing in my waist,
And the joy in my feet.
I'm a woman

Phenomenally.
Phenomenal woman,
That's me.

Men themselves have wondered
What they see in me.
They try so much
But they can't touch
My inner mystery.
When I try to show them
They say they still can't see.
I say,
It's in the arch of my back,
The sun of my smile,
The ride of my breasts,
The grace of my style.
I'm a woman
Phenomenally.
Phenomenal woman,
That's me.

Now you understand
Just why my head's not bowed.
I don't shout or jump about
Or have to talk real loud.
When you see me passing
It ought to make you proud.
I say,
It's in the click of my heels,
The bend of my hair,
the palm of my hand,

The need for my care.
'Cause I'm a woman
Phenomenally.
Phenomenal woman,
That's me.

MEN

When I was young, I used to
Watch behind the curtains
As men walked up and down
The street. Wino men, old men.
Young men sharp as mustard.
See them. Men are always
Going somewhere.
They knew I was there. Fifteen
Years old and starving for them.
Under my window, they would pause,
Their shoulders high like the
Breasts of a young girl,
Jacket tails slapping over
Those behinds,
Men.
One day they hold you in the
Palms of their hands, gentle, as if you
Were the last raw egg in the world. Then
They tighten up. Just a little. The
First squeeze is nice. A quick hug.
Soft into your defenselessness. A little
More. The hurt begins. Wrench out a
Smile that slides around the fear. When the
Air disappears,
Your mind pops, exploding fiercely, briefly,
Like the head of a kitchen match. Shattered.
It is your juice

That runs down their legs. Staining their shoes.
When the earth rights itself again,
And taste tries to return to the tongue,
Your body has slammed shut. Forever.
No keys exist.

Then the window draws full upon
Your mind. There, just beyond
The sway of curtains, men walk.
Knowing something.
Going someplace.
But this time, you will simply
Stand and watch.

Maybe.

REFUSAL

Beloved,
In what other lives or lands
Have I known your lips
Your hands
Your laughter brave
Irreverent.
Those sweet excesses that
I do adore.
What surety is there
That we will meet again,
On other worlds some
Future time undated.
I defy my body's haste.
Without the Promise
Of one more sweet encounter
I will not deign to die.

JUST FOR A TIME

Oh how you used to walk
With that insouciant smile
I liked to hear you talk
And your style
Pleased me for a while.

You were my early love
New as a day breaking in Spring
You were the image of
Everything
That caused me to sing.

I don't like reminiscing
Nostalgia is not my forté
I don't spill tears
On yesterday's years
But honesty makes me say,
You were a precious pearl
How I loved to see you shine,
You were the perfect girl.
And you were mine.
For a time.
For a time.
Just for a time.

PART TWO

Traveling

JUNKIE MONKEY REEL

Shoulders sag,
The pull of weighted needling.
Arms drag, smacking wet in soft bone
Sockets.

Knees thaw,
Their familiar magic lost. Old bend and
Lock and bend forgot.

Teeth rock in fetid gums.
Eyes dart, die, then float in
Simian juice.

Brains reel,
Master charts of old ideas erased. The
Routes are gone beneath the tracks
Of desert caravans, pre-slavery
Years ago.

Dreams fail,
Unguarded fears on homeward streets
Embrace. Throttling in a dark revenge
Murder is its sweet romance.

How long will
This monkey dance?

THE LESSON

I keep on dying again.
Veins collapse, opening like the
Small fists of sleeping
Children.
Memory of old tombs,
Rotting flesh and worms do
Not convince me against
The challenge. The years
And cold defeat live deep in
Lines along my face.
They dull my eyes, yet
I keep on dying,
Because I love to live.

CALIFORNIA PRODIGAL

for David P-B

The eye follows, the land
Slips upward, creases down, forms
The gentle buttocks of a young
Giant. In the nestle,
Old adobe bricks, washed of
Whiteness, paled to umber,
Await another century.

Star Jasmine and old vines
Lay claim upon the ghosted land,
Then quiet pools whisper
Private childhood secrets.

Flush on inner cottage walls
Antiquitous faces,
Used to the gelid breath
Of old manors, glare disdainfully
Over breached time.

Around and through these
Cold phantasmatalities,
He walks, insisting
To the languid air,
Activity, music,
A generosity of graces.

His lupin fields spurn old
Deceit and agile poppies dance
In golden riot. Each day is
Fulminant, exploding brightly
Under the gaze of his exquisite
Sires, frozen in the famed paint
Of dead masters. Audacious
Sunlight casts defiance
At their feet.

MY ARKANSAS

There is a deep brooding
in Arkansas.
Old crimes like moss pend
from poplar trees.
The sullen earth
is much too
red for comfort.

Sunrise seems to hesitate
and in that second
lose its
incandescent aim, and
dusk no more shadows
than the noon.
The past is brighter yet.

Old hates and
ante-bellum lace, are rent
but not discarded.
Today is yet to come
in Arkansas.
It writhes. It writhes in awful
waves of brooding.

THROUGH THE INNER CITY TO THE SUBURBS

Secured by sooted windows
And amazement, it is
Delicious. Frosting filched
From a company cake.

People. Black and fast. Scattered
Watermelon seeds on
A summer street. Grinning in
ritual, sassy in pomp.

From a slow moving train
They are precious. Stolen gems
Unsaleable and dear. Those
Dusky undulations sweat of forest
Nights, damp dancing, the juicy
secrets of black thighs.

Images framed picture perfect
Do not move beyond the window
Siding.

Strong delectation:
Dirty stories in changing rooms
Accompany the slap of wet towels and
Toilet seats.
Poli-talk of politician
Parents: "They need shoes and

cooze and a private
warm latrine. I had a colored
Mammy . . ."

The train, bound for green lawns
Double garages and sullen women
in dreaded homes, settles down
On its habit track.
Leaving
The dark figures dancing
And grinning. Still
Grinning.

LADY LUNCHEON CLUB

Her counsel was accepted: the times are grave.
A man was needed who would make them think,
And pay him from the petty cash account.

Our woman checked her golden watch,
The speaker has a plane to catch.
Dessert is served (and just in time).

The lecturer leans, thrusts forth his head
And neck and chest, arms akimbo
On the lectern top. He summons up
Sincerity as one might call a favored
Pet.

He understands the female rage,
Why Eve was lustful and
Delilah's
Grim deceit.

Our woman thinks:
(This cake is much too sweet.)

He sighs for youthful death
And rape at ten, and murder of
The soul stretched over long.

Our woman notes:
(This coffee's much too strong.)

The jobless streets of
Wine and wandering when
Mornings promise no bright relief.

She claps her hands and writes
Upon her pad: (Next time the
Speaker must be brief).

MOMMA WELFARE ROLL

Her arms semaphore fat triangles,
Pudgy hands bunched on layered hips
Where bones idle under years of fatback
And lima beans.
Her jowls shiver in accusation
Of crimes clichéd by
Repetition. Her children, strangers
To childhood's toys, play
Best the games of darkened doorways,
Rooftop tag, and know the slick feel of
Other people's property.

Too fat to whore,
Too mad to work,
Searches her dreams for the
Lucky sign and walks bare-handed
Into a den of bureaucrats for
Her portion.
"They don't give me welfare.
I take it."

THE SINGER WILL NOT SING

for A. L.

A benison given. Unused,
No angels promised,
wings fluttering banal lies
behind their sexlessness. No
trumpets gloried
prophecies of fabled fame.
Yet harmonies waited in
her stiff throat. New notes
lay expectant on her
stilled tongue.

Her lips are ridged and
fleshy. Purpled night birds
snuggled to rest.
The mouth seamed, voiceless,
Sounds do not lift beyond
those reddened walls.

She came too late and lonely
to this place.

WILLIE

Willie was a man without fame
Hardly anybody knew his name.
Crippled and limping, always walking lame,
He said, "I keep on movin'
Movin' just the same."

Solitude was the climate in his head
Emptiness was the partner in his bed,
Pain echoed in the steps of his tread,
He said, "I keep on followin'
Where the leaders led."

I may cry and I will die,
But my spirit is the soul of every spring,
Watch for me and you will see
That I'm present in the songs that children sing.

People called him "Uncle," "Boy" and "Hey,"
Said, "You can't live through this another day."
Then, they waited to hear what he would say.
He said, "I'm living
In the games that children play.

"You may enter my sleep, people my dreams,
Threaten my early morning's ease,
But I keep comin' followin' laughin' cryin',
Sure as a summer breeze.

"Wait for me, watch for me.
My spirit is the surge of open seas.
Look for me, ask for me,
I'm the rustle in the autumn leaves.

"When the sun rises
I am the time.
When the children sing
I am the Rhyme."

TO BEAT THE CHILD WAS BAD ENOUGH

A young body, light
As winter sunshine, a new
Seed's bursting promise,
Hung from a string of silence
Above its future.
(The chance of choice was never known.)
Hunger, new hands, strange voices,
Its cry came natural, tearing.

Water boiled in innocence, gaily
In a cheap pot.
The child exchanged its
Curiosity for terror. The skin
Withdrew, the flesh submitted.

Now, cries make shards
Of broken air, beyond an unremembered
Hunger and the peace of strange hands.

A young body floats.
Silently.

WOMAN WORK

I've got the children to tend
The clothes to mend
The floor to mop
The food to shop
Then the chicken to fry
The baby to dry
I got company to feed
The garden to weed
I've got the shirts to press
The tots to dress
The cane to be cut
I gotta clean up this hut
Then see about the sick
And the cotton to pick.

Shine on me, sunshine
Rain on me, rain
Fall softly, dewdrops
And cool my brow again.

Storm, blow me from here
With your fiercest wind
Let me float across the sky
'Til I can rest again.

Fall gently, snowflakes
Cover me with white

Cold icy kisses and
Let me rest tonight.

Sun, rain, curving sky
Mountain, oceans, leaf and stone
Star shine, moon glow
You're all that I can call my own.

ONE MORE ROUND

There ain't no pay beneath the sun
As sweet as rest when a job's well done.
I was born to work up to my grave
But I was not born
To be a slave.

One more round
And let's heave it down
One more round
And let's heave it down.

Papa drove steel and Momma stood guard,
I never heard them holler 'cause the work was hard.
They were born to work up to their graves
But they were not born
To be worked-out slaves.

One more round
And let's heave it down,
One more round
And let's heave it down.

Brothers and sisters know the daily grind,
It was not labor made them lose their minds.
They were born to work up to their graves
But they were not born
To be worked-out slaves.

One more round
And let's heave it down,
One more round
And let's heave it down.

And now I'll tell you my Golden Rule,
I was born to work but I ain't no mule.
I was born to work up to my grave
But I was not born
To be a slave.

One more round
And let's heave it down,
One more round
And let's heave it down.

THE TRAVELER

Byways and bygone
And lone nights long
Sun rays and sea waves
And star and stone

Manless and friendless
No cave my home
This is my torture
My long nights, lone

KIN

for Bailey

We were entwined in red rings
Of blood and loneliness before
The first snows fell
Before muddy rivers seeded clouds
Above a virgin forest, and
Men ran naked, blue and black
Skinned into the warm embraces
Of Sheba, Eve and Lilith.
I was your sister.

You left me to force strangers
Into brother molds, exacting
Taxations they never
Owed or could ever pay.

You fought to die, thinking
In destruction lies the seed
Of birth. You may be right.

I will remember silent walks in
Southern woods and long talks
In low voices
Shielding meaning from the big ears
Of over-curious adults.

You may be right.
Your slow return from

Regions of terror and bloody
Screams, races my heart.
I hear again the laughter
Of children and see fireflies
Bursting tiny explosion in
An Arkansas twilight.

THE MEMORY

Cotton rows crisscross the world
    And dead-tired nights of yearning
Thunderbolts on leather strops
    And all my body burning

Sugar cane reach up to God
    And every baby crying
Shame the blanket of my night
    And all my days are dying

PART THREE

And Still I Rise

STILL I RISE

You may write me down in history
With your bitter, twisted lies,
You may trod me in the very dirt
But still, like dust, I'll rise.

Does my sassiness upset you?
Why are you beset with gloom?
'Cause I walk like I've got oil wells
Pumping in my living room.

Just like moons and like suns,
With the certainty of tides,
Just like hopes springing high,
Still I'll rise.

Did you want to see me broken?
Bowed head and lowered eyes?
Shoulders falling down like teardrops,
Weakened by my soulful cries.

Does my haughtiness offend you?
Don't you take it awful hard
'Cause I laugh like I've got gold mines
Diggin' in my own back yard.

You may shoot me with your words,
You may cut me with your eyes,

You may kill me with your hatefulness,
But still, like air, I'll rise.

Does my sexiness upset you?
Does it come as a surprise
That I dance like I've got diamonds
At the meeting of my thighs?

Out of the huts of history's shame
I rise
Up from a past that's rooted in pain
I rise
I'm a black ocean, leaping and wide,
Welling and swelling I bear in the tide.

Leaving behind nights of terror and fear
I rise
Into a daybreak that's wondrously clear
I rise
Bringing the gifts that my ancestors gave,
I am the dream and the hope of the slave.
I rise
I rise
I rise.

AIN'T THAT BAD?

Dancin' the funky chicken
Eatin' ribs and tips
Diggin' all the latest sounds
And drinkin' gin in sips.

Puttin' down that do-rag
Tightenin' up my 'fro
Wrappin' up in Blackness
Don't I shine and glow?

Hearin' Stevie Wonder
Cookin' beans and rice
Goin' to the opera
Checkin' out Leontyne Price.

Get down, Jesse Jackson
Dance on, Alvin Ailey
Talk, Miss Barbara Jordan
Groove, Miss Pearlie Bailey.

Now ain't they bad?
An' ain't they Black?
An' ain't they Black?
An' ain't they Bad?
An' ain't they bad?
An' ain't they Black?
An' ain't they fine?

Black like the hour of the night
When your love turns and wriggles close to your side
Black as the earth which has given birth
To nations, and when all else is gone will abide.

Bad as the storm that leaps raging from the heavens
Bringing the welcome rain
Bad as the sun burning orange hot at midday
Lifting the waters again.

Arthur Ashe on the tennis court
Mohammed Ali in the ring
André Watts and Andrew Young
Black men doing their thing.

Dressing in purples and pinks and greens
Exotic as rum and Cokes
Living our lives with flash and style
Ain't we colorful folks?

Now ain't we bad?
An' ain't we Black?
An' ain't we Black?
An' ain't we bad?
An' ain't we bad?
An' ain't we Black?
An' ain't we fine?

LIFE DOESN'T FRIGHTEN ME

Shadows on the wall
Noises down the hall
Life doesn't frighten me at all
Bad dogs barking loud
Big ghosts in a cloud
Life doesn't frighten me at all.

Mean old Mother Goose
Lions on the loose
They don't frighten me at all
Dragons breathing flame
On my counterpane
That doesn't frighten me at all,

I go boo
Make them shoo
I make fun
Way they run
I won't cry
So they fly
I just smile
They go wild
Life doesn't frighten me at all.

Tough guys in a fight
All alone at night
Life doesn't frighten me at all.

Panthers in the park
Strangers in the dark
No, they don't frighten me at all.

That new classroom where
Boys all pull my hair
(Kissy little girls
With their hair in curls)
They don't frighten me at all.

Don't show me frogs and snakes
And listen for my scream,
If I'm afraid at all
It's only in my dreams.

I've got a magic charm
That I keep up my sleeve,
I can walk the ocean floor
And never have to breathe.

Life doesn't frighten me at all
Not at all
Not at all.
Life doesn't frighten me at all.

BUMP D'BUMP

Play me a game like Blind Man's dance
And bind my eyes with ignorance
Bump d'bump bump d'bump.

Tell my life with a liquor sign
Or a cooking spoon from the five-and-dime
And a junkie reel in two/four time
Bump d'bump bump d'bump.

Call me a name from an ugly south
Like liver lips and satchel mouth
Bump d'bump bump d'bump.

I'll play possum and close my eyes
To your greater sins and my lesser lies
That way I share my nation's prize
Bump d'bump bump d'bump.

I may be last in the welfare line
Below the rim where the sun don't shine
But getting up stays on my mind
Bump d'bump bump d'bump.

ON AGING

When you see me sitting quietly,
Like a sack left on the shelf,
Don't think I need your chattering.
I'm listening to myself.
Hold! Stop! Don't pity me!
Hold! Stop your sympathy!
Understanding if you got it,
Otherwise I'll do without it!

When my bones are stiff and aching
And my feet won't climb the stair,
I will only ask one favor:
Don't bring me no rocking chair.

When you see me walking, stumbling,
Don't study and get it wrong.
'Cause tired don't mean lazy
And every goodbye ain't gone.
I'm the same person I was back then,
A little less hair, a little less chin,
A lot less lungs and much less wind.
But ain't I lucky I can still breathe in.

IN RETROSPECT

Last year changed its seasons
subtly, stripped its sultry winds
for the reds of dying leaves, let
gelid drips of winter ice melt onto a
warming earth and urged the dormant
bulbs to brave the
pain of spring.

We, loving, above the whim of
time, did not notice.

Alone. I remember now.

JUST LIKE JOB

My Lord, My Lord,
Long have I cried out to Thee
In the heat of the sun,
The cool of the moon,
My screams searched the heavens for Thee.
My God,
When my blanket was nothing but dew,
Rags and bones
Were all I owned.
I chanted Your name
Just like Job.

Father, Father,
My life give I gladly to Thee
Deep rivers ahead
High mountains above
My soul wants only Your love
But fears gather round like wolves in the dark
Have You forgotten my name?
Oh, Lord, come to Your child.
Oh, Lord, forget me not.

You said to lean on Your arm
And I'm leaning
You said to trust in Your love
And I'm trusting
You said to call on Your name

And I'm calling
I'm stepping out on Your word.

You said You'd be my protection,
My only and glorious saviour
My beautiful Rose of Sharon,
And I'm stepping out on Your word.
Joy, joy
Your word.
Joy, joy
The wonderful word of the Son of God.

You said that You would take me to glory
To sit down at the welcome table
Rejoice with my mother in heaven
And I'm stepping out on Your word.

Into the alleys
Into the byways
Into the streets
And the roads
And the highways
Past rumor mongers
And midnight ramblers
Past the liars and the cheaters and the gamblers
On Your word
On Your word.
On the wonderful word of the Son of God.
I'm stepping out on Your word.

CALL LETTERS: MRS. V.B.

Ships?
Sure I'll sail them.
Show me the boat,
If it'll float,
I'll sail it.

Men?
Yes I'll love them.
If they've got the style,
To make me smile,
I'll love them.

Life?
'Course I'll live it.
Let me have breath,
Just to my death,
And I'll live it.

Failure?
I'm not ashamed to tell it,
I never learned to spell it.
Not Failure.

THANK YOU, LORD

I see You
Brown-skinned,
Neat Afro,
Full lips,
A little goatee.
A Malcolm,
Martin,
Du Bois.
Sunday services become sweeter when you're Black,
Then I don't have to explain why
I was out balling the town down,
Saturday night.

Thank you, Lord.
I want to thank You, Lord
For life and all that's in it.
Thank You for the day
And for the hour and for the minute.
I know many are gone,
I'm still living on,
I want to thank You.

I went to sleep last night
And I arose with the dawn,
I know that there are others
Who're still sleeping on,
They've gone away,

You've let me stay.
I want to thank You.

Some thought because they'd seen sunrise
They'd see it rise again.
But death crept into their sleeping beds
And took them by the hand.
Because of Your mercy,
I have another day to live.

Let me humbly say,
Thank You for this day
I want to thank You.

I was once a sinner man,
Living unsaved and wild,
Taking my chances in a dangerous world,
Putting my soul on trial.
Because of Your mercy,
Falling down on me like rain,
Because of Your mercy,
When I die I'll live again,
Let me humbly say,
Thank You for this day.
I want to thank You.

SHAKER WHY DON'T YOU SING?

Another book for
GUY JOHNSON
and
COLIN ASHANTI MURPHY JOHNSON

Thanks to

ELEANOR TRAYLOR for her radiance

ELIZABETH PHILLIPS for her art

RUTH BECKFORD for her constancy

AWAKING IN NEW YORK

Curtains forcing their will
against the wind,
children sleep,
exchanging dreams with
seraphim. The city
drags itself awake on
subway straps; and
I, an alarm, awake as a
rumor of war,
lay stretching into dawn,
unasked and unheeded.

A GOOD WOMAN FEELING BAD

The blues may be the life you've led
Or midnight hours in
An empty bed. But persecuting
Blues I've known
Could stalk
Like tigers, break like bone,

Pend like rope in
A gallows tree,
Make me curse
My pedigree,

Bitterness thick on
A rankling tongue,
A psalm to love that's
Left unsung,

Rivers heading north
But ending South,
Funeral music
In a going-home mouth.

All riddles are blues,
And all blues are sad,
And I'm only mentioning
Some blues I've had.

THE HEALTH-FOOD DINER

No sprouted wheat and soya shoots
And Brussels in a cake,
Carrot straw and spinach raw,
(Today, I need a steak).

Not thick brown rice and rice pilau
Or mushrooms creamed on toast,
Turnips mashed and parsnips hashed,
(I'm dreaming of a roast).

Health-food folks around the world
Are thinned by anxious zeal,
They look for help in seafood kelp
(I count on breaded veal).

No Smoking signs, raw mustard greens,
Zucchini by the ton,
Uncooked kale and bodies frail
Are sure to make me run

to

Loins of pork and chicken thighs
And standing rib, so prime,
Pork chops brown and fresh ground round
(I crave them all the time).

Irish stews and boiled corned beef
and hot dogs by the scores,
or any place that saves a space
For smoking carnivores.

A GEORGIA SONG

We swallow the odors of Southern cities,
Fat back boiled to submission,
Tender evening poignancies of
Magnolia and the great green
Smell of fresh sweat.
In Southern fields,
The sound of distant
Feet running, or dancing,
And the liquid notes of
Sorrow songs,
Waltzes, screams and
French quadrilles float over
The loam of Georgia.

Sing me to sleep, Savannah.

Clocks run down in Tara's halls and dusty
Flags droop their unbearable
Sadness.

Remember our days, Susannah.

Oh, the blood-red clay,
Wet still with ancient
Wrongs, and Abenaa
Singing her Creole airs to
Macon.
We long, dazed, for winter evenings
And a whitened moon,
And the snap of controllable fires.

Cry for our souls, Augusta.

We need a wind to strike
Sharply, as the thought of love
Betrayed can stop the heart.
An absence of tactile
Romance, no lips offering
Succulence, nor eyes
Rolling, disconnected from
A Sambo face.

Dare us new dreams, Columbus.

A cool new moon, a
Winter's night, calm blood,
Sluggish, moving only
Out of habit, we need
Peace.

Oh Atlanta, oh deep, and
Once lost city,

Chant for us a new song. A song
Of Southern peace.

UNMEASURED TEMPO

The sun rises at midday.
Nubile breasts sag to waistlines while
young loins grow dull,
so late.
Dreams are petted, like
cherished lap dogs
misunderstood and loved
too well.

Much knowledge
wrinkles the cerebellum,
but little informs.
Leaps are
made into narrow mincings.
Great desires strain
into petty wishes.
You did arrive, smiling,
but too late.

AMOEBAEAN FOR DADDY

I was a pretty baby.
White folks used to stop
My mother
Just to look at me.
(All black babies
Are Cute). Mother called me
Bootsie and Daddy said . . .
(Nobody listened to him).

On the Union Pacific, a
Dining-car waiter, bowing and scraping,
Momma told him to
Stand up straight, he shamed her
In the big house
(Bought from tips) in front of her
Nice club ladies.

His short legs were always
Half bent. He could have posed as
The Black jockey Mother found
And put on the lawn.
He sat silent when
We ate from the good railroad china

And stolen silver spoons.
Furniture crowded our
Lonely house.

But I was young and played
In the evenings under a blanket of
Licorice sky. When Daddy came home
(I might be forgiven) that last night,
I had been running in the
Big back yard and
Stood sweating above the tired old man,
Panting like a young horse,
Impatient with his lingering. He said
"All I ever asked, all I ever asked, all I ever—"
Daddy, you should have died
Long before I was a
Pretty baby, and white
Folks used to stop
Just to look at me.

RECOVERY

for Dugald

A last love,
proper in conclusion,
should snip the wings
forbidding further flight.

But I, now,
reft of that confusion,
am lifted up
and speeding toward the light.

IMPECCABLE CONCEPTION

I met a Lady Poet
who took for inspiration
colored birds, and whispered words,
a lover's hesitation.

A falling leaf could stir her.
A wilting, dying rose
would make her write, both day and night,
the most rewarding prose.

She'd find a hidden meaning
in every pair of pants,
then hurry home to be alone
and write about romance.

CAGED BIRD

A free bird leaps
on the back of the wind
and floats downstream
till the current ends
and dips his wing
in the orange sun rays
and dares to claim the sky.

But a bird that stalks
down his narrow cage
can seldom see through
his bars of rage
his wings are clipped and
his feet are tied
so he opens his throat to sing.

The caged bird sings
with a fearful trill
of things unknown
but longed for still
and his tune is heard
on the distant hill

for the caged bird
sings of freedom.

The free bird thinks of another breeze
and the trade winds soft through the sighing trees
and the fat worms waiting on a dawn-bright lawn
and he names the sky his own.

But a caged bird stands on the grave of dreams
his shadow shouts on a nightmare scream
his wings are clipped and his feet are tied
so he opens his throat to sing.

The caged bird sings
with a fearful trill
of things unknown
but longed for still
and his tune is heard
on the distant hill
for the caged bird
sings of freedom.

AVEC MERCI, MOTHER

From her perch of beauty
posing lofty,
Sustained upon the plaudits
of the crowd,

She praises all who kneel and
whispers softly,
"A genuflection's better
with head bowed."

Among the mass of people
who adore her
A solitary figure
holds her eyes.

His salty tears invoke
her sweet reaction,
"He's so much like his daddy
when he cries."

ARRIVAL

Angels gather.
The rush of mad air
cyclones through.
Wing tips brush the
hair, a million
strands
stand; waving black anemones.
Hosannahs crush the
shell's ear tender, and
tremble
down clattering
to the floor.
Harps sound,
undulate their
sensuous meanings.
Hallelujah! Hallelujah!
You
beyond the door.

A PLAGUED JOURNEY

There is no warning rattle at the door
nor heavy feet to stomp the foyer boards.
safe in the dark prison, I know that
light slides over
the fingered work of a toothless
woman in Pakistan.
Happy prints of
an invisible time are illumined.
My mouth agape
rejects the solid air and
lungs hold. The invader takes
direction and
seeps through the plaster walls.
It is at my chamber entering
the keyhole, pushing
through the padding of the door.
I cannot scream. A bone
of fear clogs my throat.
It is upon me. It is
sunrise, with Hope
its arrogant rider.
My mind, formerly quiescent
in its snug encasement, is strained

to look upon their rapturous visages,
to let them enter even into me.
I am forced
outside myself to
mount the light and ride joined with Hope.

Through all the bright hours
I cling to expectation, until
darkness comes to reclaim me
as its own. Hope fades, day is gone
into its irredeemable place
and I am thrown back into the familiar
bonds of disconsolation.
Gloom crawls around
lapping lasciviously
between my toes, at my ankles,
and it sucks the strands of my
hair. It forgives my heady
fling with Hope. I am
joined again into its
greedy arms.

STARVATION

Hurray! Hurry!
Come through the keyhole.
Don't mind the rotting
sashes, pass into the windows.
Come, good news.

I'm holding my apron to
catch your plumpness.
The largest pot shines
with happiness. The slack
walls of my purse, pulsing
pudenda, await you with
a new bride's longing.
The bread bin gapes and
the oven holds its cold
breath.
Hurry up! Hurry down!
Good tidings. Don't wait
out my misery. Do not play
coy with my longing.

Hunger has grown old and
ugly with me. We hate from

too much knowing. Come.
Press out this sour beast which
fills the bellies of my children
and laughs at each eviction notice.
Come!

CONTEMPORARY ANNOUNCEMENT

Ring the big bells,
cook the cow,
put on your silver locket.
The landlord is knocking at the door
and I've got the rent in my pocket.

Douse the lights,
Hold your breath,
take my heart in your hand.
I lost my job two weeks ago
and rent day's here again.

PRELUDE TO A PARTING

Beside you, prone,
my naked skin finds
fault in touching.
Yet it is you
who draws away.
The tacit fact is:
the awful fear of losing
is not enough to cause
a fleeing love
to stay.

MARTIAL CHOREOGRAPH

Hello young sailor.
You are betrayed and
do not know the dance of death.
Dandy warrior, swaying to
Rick James on your
stereo, you do not hear the
bleat of triumphant war, its
roar is not in
your ears, filled with Stevie Wonder.

"Show me how to do like you.
Show me how to do it."

You will be surprised that
trees grunt when torn from
their root sockets to fandango into dust,
and exploding bombs force a lively Lindy
on grasses and frail bodies.

Go galloping on, bopping,
in the airport, young sailor.
Your body, virgin
still, has not swung the bloody buck and wing.

Manhood is a newly delivered
message. Your eyes,
rampant as an open city,
have not yet seen life steal from
limbs outstretched and trembling
like the arms of dancers
and dying swans.

TO A SUITOR

If you are Black and for me,
press steady, as the weight
of night. And I will show
cascades of brilliance, astrally.

If you are Black and constant,
descend importantly,
as ritual, and I will arch
a crescent moon, naturally.

INSOMNIAC

There are some nights when
sleep plays coy,
aloof and disdainful.
And all the wiles
that I employ to win
its service to my side
are useless as wounded pride,
and much more painful.

WEEKEND GLORY

Some dichty folks
don't know the facts,
posin' and preenin'
and puttin' on acts,
stretchin' their necks
and strainin' their backs.

They move into condos
up over the ranks,
pawn their souls
to the local banks.
Buying big cars
they can't afford,
ridin' around town
actin' bored.

If they want to learn how to live life right,
they ought to study me on Saturday night.

My job at the plant
ain't the biggest bet,
but I pay my bills
and stay out of debt.

I get my hair done
for my own self's sake,
so I don't have to pick
and I don't have to rake.

Take the church money out
and head cross town
to my friend girl's house
where we plan our round.
We meet our men and go to a joint
where the music is blues
and to the point.

Folks write about me.
They just can't see
how I work all week
at the factory.
Then get spruced up
and laugh and dance
And turn away from worry
with sassy glance.

They accuse me of livin'
from day to day,
but who are they kiddin'?
So are they.

My life ain't heaven
but it sure ain't hell.
I'm not on top
but I call it swell
if I'm able to work
and get paid right
and have the luck to be Black
on a Saturday night.

THE LIE

Today, you threaten to leave me.
I hold curses, in my mouth,
which could flood your path, sear
bottomless chasms in your road.

I keep, behind my lips,
invectives capable of tearing
the septum from your
nostrils and the skin from your back.

Tears, copious as a spring rain,
are checked in ducts
and screams are crowded in a corner
of my throat.

You are leaving?

Aloud, I say:
I'll help you pack, but it's getting late,
I have to hurry or miss my date.
When I return, I know you'll be gone.
Do drop a line or telephone.

PRESCIENCE

Had I known that the heart
breaks slowly, dismantling itself
into unrecognizable plots of
misery,

Had I known the heart would leak,
slobbering its sap, with a vulgar
visibility, into the dressed-up
dining rooms of strangers,

Had I known that solitude could
stifle the breath, loosen the joint,
and force the tongue against the
palate,

Had I known that loneliness could
keloid, winding itself around the
body in an ominous and beautiful
cicatrix,

Had I known yet I would have loved
you, your brash and insolent beauty,
your heavy comedic face

and knowledge of sweet
delights,

But from a distance
I would have left you whole and wholly
for the delectation of those who
wanted more and cared less.

FAMILY AFFAIRS

You let down, from arched
Windows,
Over hand-cut stones of your
Cathedrals, seas of golden hair.

While I, pulled by dusty braids,
Left furrows in the
Sands of African beaches.

Princes and commoners
Climbed over waves to reach
Your vaulted boudoirs,

As the sun, capriciously,
Struck silver fire from waiting
Chains, where I was bound.

My screams never reached
The rare tower where you
Lay, birthing masters for
My sons, and for my
Daughters, a swarm of

Unclean badgers, to consume
Their history.

Tired now of pedestal existence
For fear of flying
And vertigo, you descend
And step lightly over
My centuries of horror
And take my hand,

Smiling call me
        Sister.

Sister, accept
That I must wait a
While. Allow an age
Of dust to fill
Ruts left on my
Beach in Africa.

CHANGES

Fickle comfort steals away
What it knows
It will not say
What it can
It will not do
It flies from me
To humor you.

Capricious peace will not bind
The severed nerves
The jagged mind
The shattered dream
The loveless sleep
It frolics now
Within your keep.

Confidence, that popinjay,
Is planning now
To slip away
Look fast
It's fading rapidly
Tomorrow it returns to me.

BRIEF INNOCENCE

Dawn offers
innocence to a half-mad city.

The axe-keen
intent of all our
days for this brief
moment lies soft, nuzzling
the breast of morning,
crooning, still sleep-besotted,
of childish pranks with
angels.

THE LAST DECISION

The print is too small, distressing me.
Wavering black things on the page.
Wriggling polliwogs all about.
I know it's my age.
I'll have to give up reading.

The food is too rich, revolting me.
I swallow it hot or force it down cold,
and wait all day as it sits in my throat.
Tired as I am, I know I've grown old.
I'll have to give up eating.

My children's concerns are tiring me.
They stand at my bed and move their lips,
and I cannot hear one single word.
I'd rather give up listening.

Life is too busy, wearying me.
Questions and answers and heavy thought.
I've subtracted and added and multiplied,
and all my figuring has come to naught.
Today I'll give up living.

SLAVE COFFLE

Just Beyond my reaching,
  an itch away from fingers,
  was the river bed
  and the high road home.

Now Beneath my walking,
  solid down to China,
  all the earth is horror
  and the dark night long.

Then Before the dawning,
  bright as grinning demons,
  came the fearful knowledge
  that my life was gone.

SHAKER, WHY DON'T YOU SING?

Evicted from sleep's mute palace,
I wait in silence
for the bridal croon;
your legs rubbing insistent
rhythm against my thighs,
your breast moaning
a canticle in my hair.
But the solemn moments,
unuttering, pass in
unaccompanied procession.
You, whose chanteys hummed
my life alive, have withdrawn
your music and lean inaudibly
on the quiet slope of memory.

O Shaker, why don't you sing?

In the night noisome with
street cries and the triumph

of amorous insects, I focus beyond
those cacophonies for
the anthem of your hands and swelling chest,
for the perfect harmonies which are
your lips. Yet darkness brings
no syncopated promise. I rest somewhere
between the unsung notes of night.

Shaker, why don't you sing?

MY LIFE HAS TURNED TO BLUE

Our summer's gone,
the golden days are through.
The rosy dawns I used to
wake with you
have turned to gray,
my life has turned to blue.

The once-green lawns
glisten now with dew.
Red robin's gone,
down to the South he flew.
Left here alone,
my life has turned to blue.

I've heard the news
that winter too will pass,
that spring's a sign
that summer's due at last.
But until I see you
lying in green grass,
my life has turned to blue.

[*100*